The Boy from Illinois

By Leland K. Good

ISBN-10: 1503103145
ISBN-13: 978-1503103146

Word of Thanks

I want to express my appreciation to Marie Good,
one of the greatest daughters-in-law I've been blessed with,
for her help, guidance, and encouragement in producing this book.

~ Leland Good

Table of Contents

It's a Boy

It was 1938. Ivan and Lu Ella Conrad Good were settled into farm life near the town of Rantoul, Illinois -- a busy town, with a large military air base. They had five children, and worked hard to support the family. They attended (and were members of) the East Bend Mennonite Church.

Lu Ella had not been feeling well, so was admitted to the local hospital. The doctors decided to investigate the possible tumor in her pelvic area. To everyone's surprise, they found a baby growing naturally in the proper place. On December 14, Lu Ella delivered a baby boy in the downstairs bedroom of their home at Route 2, Rantoul, Illinois. They gave him the name Leland Kenneth Good.

Because Leland wasn't doing well, Dr. Troyer was concerned enough that he invited Lu Ella and the baby to live with him and his wife for several weeks so he could observe what was going on. The doctor discovered Leland had a problem with milk intolerance, so was given goats milk, which he was able to drink. Leland continued to grow up sort of small and thin. Around the age of ten, his parents purchased some vitamins from a cousin for him to take. The result was a success. Leland began to grow and catch up with his peers.

I am Leland. From this point in the story, I will write in my own words.

Boys will be Boys

About two-and-a-half years after my birth, another little boy, Loren Conrad, was born on July 20, 1941. We grew up together, and were almost the same size. Many people took us to be twins. Life was good. We had wonderful loving parents, and a happy family life. Often after the evening meal, Papa would call us into

1

the living room to sing around the piano. One of my sisters played the piano. At first I didn't enjoy this activity, but as I grew older, I learned to enjoy singing too. My father and his three brothers sang together as a men's quartet. When Loren and I got older, we and our two older brothers also sang together as a men's quartet.

One summer during hay-making season, the machinery was set up in front of the barn. The hay was cut in the field, and then raked into wind rows to dry. A machine called a hay chopper picked up the hay, chopped it into small pieces, and blew it back into a large wagon. The wagon was taken to the barn, and the hay was raked by hand out of the back of the wagon, into a machine called a hay blower. The blower had a conveyer to move the hay into the fan that blew the hay up into the haymow of the barn. There were two chains running the full length of the conveyer, with metal straps attached to both chains, spaced every twelve inches or so, to help move the hay into the blower. When the blower was not being used, the conveyer was lifted up into the vertical position. My brother and I thought this would make a wonderful "elevator" to ride up and down on. I held on to one iron strap, and put my feet on another strap below. My brother Loren put the machine in gear and turned it by hand, lifting me up on our "elevator." All went well, until the machine worked itself out of gear, causing me to fall down, hitting the metal prongs that kept the hay level as it was fed into the blower. Unfortunately, one of the prongs tore a big hole in my behind. That stopped the work while I was taken to the doctor's office to get the hole sewed back together. It was many days before I could sit comfortably again. I can only imagine my Father's anger and disgust with us boys for fooling around while they were busy working. As I remember however, Papa did not even scold us.

A Boy and His Papa

Papa was an amazing man of God. One time, when he and I were working in the hay mow, he decided to crawl up the wall using the 4 x 4 cross members instead of a ladder. He was up about fifteen feet, when he lost his grip on the cross member and fell backwards, landing on his behind on the wooden floor. I can see it in my mind's eye even now. As I can remember, he just got up, dusted himself off, and went about his work without so much as a comment.

Another time he had me hold the wagon hitch up, while he backed the tractor to hook it to the wagon. He held the hitch pin in one hand, while leaning backward over the seat to drop the pin into the holes when they lined up, connecting the wagon with the tractor. He steered with his other hand, and with one foot controlled the movement of the tractor. The tractor jumped or something happened, and caught his thumb between the hitch and the tractor, smashing his thumb flat. It was bleeding and looked terrible. Papa never said a word, just went to the house to get it cleaned up. I never ever saw him get angry or use foul language.

Country School

For my first three years of school, I attended a one-room country school. We lived one-and-a-half miles from the school, so we walked to and from school most every day. One day during school, it was terrible cold and windy. During the day it began to snow, and turned into a blizzard. When school dismissed and no one came to pick us up, my older sister, Bernelle, and I started walking home. It was so cold. We had walked about half way home when here came Papa walking to meet us. It was so cold, the car wouldn't start. He then walked ahead of us, facing the wind, then my sister walked behind him, and I followed last, behind her.

Our teacher taught all eight grades. In the winter, she would have to fire up the wood stove when she arrived at school before she could start teaching. Sometimes it was so cold in the school, the bigger boys would climb up and sit on top of the stove where it was warm. The rest of us little kids and the girls stood around the stove until the room heated up. We played outside at recess and at noon.   Sometimes the teacher would even come out and play games or soft ball with us.   One of the older boys didn't always smell too good - who knows, maybe his house was too cold to take a bath in.   Everyone called him "Stinky Albers."   Being a little kid, and not knowing any better, I called him that to his face.   He chased me around the school yard until he caught me, and then pounded on me until I yelled.

Sometimes in the winter time, during lunch hour, we would walk the half mile to the creek to go ice skating, or play ice hockey with sticks and a tin can.

I remember when Papa decided to stop milking cows and have an auction; they closed school for the day, because almost all of the students were planning to attend the auction.

The teacher wasn't much older than the older boys attending school.   Sometimes the "big" boys weren't very nice to the teacher, and wouldn't obey.   I remember seeing her cry, because they wouldn't obey her and she didn't know what to do.

When she was teaching me to read, we had a story of some children going to the park to play.   I was trying to read the story. When I came to the word "park," I didn't know how to pronounce it.   The teacher was from the east coast, or the south, or *somewhere*, so had an accent different then we in Central Illinois. She told me to pronounce the word as, "pak." That evening when I was reading the story to Papa, I read, "The kids went to the "pak" to play."   Papa quickly told me how to pronounce the word correctly.

When I reached fourth grade, I went to a larger school in the town of Dewey.   Beginning with the sixth grade, I attended Fisher Community School, in the small town of Fisher, Illinois. I graduated from high school in the spring of 1957. I didn't have a very good image of myself during my school years, thinking I was kind of dumb and backward. My grades were average, but not real good.   But, I was successful in typing class, played the trombone,

4

sang in the choir and solo and small group competitions, where I won red and blue ribbons. I enjoyed being part of the junior and senior class plays, playing the part of a policeman in one play. I took an agriculture class and had sheep for a project. I also raised and sold Toy Manchester dogs. The most enjoyable class was woodworking shop. That class started me on a lifetime journey of working with wood in various ways.

There was a classmate in shop class whose name was Roy. We were friends, but he just kept picking on me, teasing me, and tricking me all the time. Perhaps he would move the material I was working with just to bother me. One day he did something again while I was working on my project. On the table next to where I was working was a 2 X 4 about four feet long. I grabbed that 2 X 4 and hit him on his behind as hard as I could. Boy was he ever surprised. He never bothered me again, and we continued to be best friends throughout school.

A Boy and His Lord

Mama and Papa always took us to church - usually Sunday morning and evening, and most every Wednesday night prayer meeting. I'm not real sure, but somewhere around the age of twelve, there was an evangelist speaking at our church every evening for a week or so. One of those evenings, I felt the Holy Spirit calling me to accept Jesus as my Lord and Savior. That began a lifelong walk of serving the Lord to the best of my ability and understanding. I remember one time in church, I was carrying my Bible. Uncle Lester Hershey said to me, "I'm glad to see you brought your Bible with you." He encouraged me to bring it with me every time. That simple bit of encouragement has always stayed with me. From then on, I have always carried my Bible, and enjoy following along when it is being read.

A Boy and His Cousin

After graduation from high school, I worked for my brother-in-law, Jasper Roth. He built and sold homes in the Dewey and Champaign Urbana, Illinois area. I think he paid me $1.25 per hour, and we did every kind of job connected with the building business.

Evenings were free, so I attended youth group activities and other fun things. I had a favorite cousin, Arlynn McGinnis, who lived about an hour away. Most every summer she would come stay with Uncle Wayne and Aunt Elma Tarvin for a week or so. Like I said, evenings were free, so often, my brother Loren, and Arlynn and I would go do something together. One time there was a carnival in the neighboring town. Now remember, good Mennonites didn't make it a habit of attending such worldly things. However, we decided to go check it out. Surely it wasn't so bad a thing to do. One of the booths there had a game where you just rolled a little ball over a hump and if it went into the hole, you won a prize. It was so easy, and really didn't hurt anything to try, and I got so close to winning. Soon all my money was gone, and we decided to go back the next night to try again to win a prize. Soon my money was gone again, and still no prize. I have always remembered that lesson throughout life, and have never again played those games. You can be sure we never told our parents of our walk off of the straight-and-narrow path.

Arlynn and I enjoyed playing tricks on each other, and that continues today. She came to visit one summer, and stayed at our house overnight. I took an alarm clock, set it for 3:00 a.m., and put it under the bed she would sleep in. At 3:00 in the morning it rang and rang, and she had a hard time finding it to shut it off. Nothing much was said about it, until I came home from work the next afternoon. We were going to go out for the evening again, so I ran upstairs to shower and clean up. Unknown to me, she had looked in my bedroom during the day, and noticed where I had sat on the bed to put on my shoes. She took four thumb tacks and placed them under the spread where I had sat that morning. You guessed it; I sat down in the exact same place, and sat right on top of all four tacks. It didn't take me long to stand back up.

6

Another time, after we were both married "adults," we attended the Conrad reunion. Arlynn lived in Kansas, and I lived in Ohio, but both families were able to attend the reunion in Illinois. Arlynn brought what looked like a flower pot filled with a chocolate dessert that had an imitation flower growing in it. It was called "Kansas Dirt." Now chocolate dessert of any kind is good, so I helped myself to a good serving of it. As I was enjoying the dessert, all at once I found what I thought was a fish worm. I gagged, and almost threw up! Looking across the room, I seen Arlynn laughing herself silly. She had put a gummy worm into the dessert, hoping I would find it. Somehow that trick had worked out great for her.

Boy Meets Girl

In the fall of 1957, I enrolled for general courses at Goshen College, Goshen, Indiana. Tuition for each semester cost $425.00, including room and board. Again, much like high school, I didn't do well in my studies, so at the end of the first semester I opted to take some elective classes for the remainder of the year, deciding not to return to school another year. I did make lots of friends with lots of classmates that have lasted a lifetime. Oh yes, don't forget the cute girls in the freshman class. I really dreaded going to civilization class. It was so boring, but the professor had us sit in alphabetic order. My name is Good, and several seats down was a really cute girl with the name Deloris Graber. We began seeing each other out of class, attending concerts, or going for ice cream. During the following summer, I made several weekend trips, driving six hours to Archbold, Ohio, to visit her.

A Boy's Duty to Serve (Becoming a Man)

During those years, at eighteen years of age, all young men had to register with the government for Selective Service in the military. Traditionally, the Mennonite church believed and taught that military service violated the Bible's teaching to "love your neighbor as yourself," to "be kind one to another," and to "turn the other cheek when someone strikes you, and don't retaliate." Because of this longstanding belief, the government offered those of us who were "consciences objectors to military service" the opportunity to serve in an alternative service program, administered by the church. Those serving under this program were given credit for the two years of service to the government required by all young men. These programs were designated under several names, including: I-W, Voluntary Service, and PAX programs.

Near the end of the 1958 school year, Mennonite Central Committee (the service agency of the Mennonite church) contacted me, offering a service opportunity to work at a leprosy hospital compound in Ban Mê Thuột, Vietnam. The only unusual requirement about this service project was a three-year commitment, due to the geographical distance, opposed to the required two-year requirement to satisfy the government. In praying and thinking about this offer, I soon felt it was something the Lord wanted me to do. I was told to report to Akron, Pennsylvania in August. My family and I quickly began to prepare for this move, and to collect clothes and needed items for the next three years. There would be no time allowed to return home for a visit, due to the distance and the long travel time involved. I was informed, in this "strange" land, I might encounter things like big spiders, poisonous snakes, and wild animals -- including tigers and other fearful critters.

During that summer, I worked for my brother in law, Jasper Roth, and made several trips to Ohio to visit Deloris Graber, my girl friend. When all was ready, my parents and younger brother drove me to Akron, Pennsylvania, stopping in Archbold, Ohio for one last visit with Deloris, the daughter of Raymond and Mildred Graber. The following day we headed on to Akron for the several days of orientation. The next day I remember like it was yesterday -- standing on the sidewalk, saying goodbye to my parents. I was only eighteen years old, and we would not see one another again for three years. I don't know how my parents could cope with all the emotions involved in that moment.

S.S. Statendam

The trip over to Vietnam took most of a month of travel time. There were five of us young men. Two were heading for an assignment to Nepal. The other three of us were headed to Vietnam. We sailed out of New York on August 29, 1958 on the S.S. Statendam, a beautiful passenger ship, stopping briefly at South Hampton, England, then sailing on to Le Havre, France.

We were five country boys, on an upscale sailing vessel. There were a thousand passengers on board, with all sorts of activities to enjoy. Twice a day they served tea in a lounge, while musicians played stringed instruments to entertain the guests. We were informed we were required to wear a coat to the dining room. On the first visit to the dining room, we found four or five utensils on either side of the plate, and several more above the plate. Besides that, we found a large envelope beside each plate. We country boys didn't have a clue how to use all that silverware, or what the envelope might be for. After much discussion, we each put several dollars "tip" into our envelope. When we arrived for the next meal, we found our cloth napkin neatly folded and inserted inside the envelope. I can only imagine the laughter we caused the waiters, because of those "simple country boys."

Five days later, on September 3, we arrived in France and visited several days in Paris. Several of the MCC personal working there took us around to see the sights of the city, including the Louvre museum, the Arc de Triomphe, and the Eiffel Tower.

S.S. Vietnam

We then traveled by train to Marseille, France, where we boarded a French passenger ship, the S. S. Vietnam. This ship was not as plush as the first ship, and not nearly as large. The food was French, and very different than what we were used to. They served beautiful looking steaks, but they were so rare we didn't enjoy them, and everyone drank red wine with the meal, like we drink coffee. They couldn't understand why we only wanted to drink water with the meal.

One of the passengers was a pretty young French girl who looked very much like my girl friend, Deloris. I did not talk to her, but I watched her some, because of her resemblance of Deloris. There was a swimming pool up on the top deck of the ship. One day several of us fellas decided to go for a swim. When we got up to the pool, the only one in the pool was this pretty French girl. She swam back and forth, back and forth, under the water before coming up for a breath of air. She was wearing the littlest, teeny weenie bikini we country boys had ever seen. We promptly turned around and went back to our room, not knowing what else to do.

Now, let's jump ahead four-five years for a bit. When I returned to the USA, Deloris and I married. It was then I learned her father, Raymond Graber, was of French decent, from the area of Alsace-Lorraine. Every several years, a relative from France, Andre Goll, with his wife, would come visit Raymond and Mildred. What are the chances, do you suppose, that the pretty French girl, who looked and acted similar to Deloris, might have been a distant relative ... a cousin of some kind?

The ship sailed through the Mediterranean Sea, the Suez Canal, and the Red sea. The Mediterranean Sea was a beautiful blue color, and was very smooth. From the deck we could watch bright blue fish about twenty-four inches long with twelve-inch, bright yellow wings/fins, jump out of the water and sail through the air for several feet. We saw places like Sicily, Italy, Mt. Stromboli, a volcanic island, and some islands off Greece as we sailed towards Egypt. This was in the area where Paul from the Bible traveled on his missionary journeys. We stopped at Aden, and Bombay, India, where the two fellas who were headed to Nepal to work, got off the ship. We continued on, stopping at Colombo, Ceylon, and on to Singapore, where we stopped to pick up our visas for Vietnam.

When the ship stopped at Port Said, Egypt, before sailing through the Suez Canal, we took a day-and-a-half side trip to Cairo, Egypt to see the Sphinx and the pyramids. The cost was $31.00 -- almost too expensive to even consider -- but we decided we may never pass this way again. We rode around on camel back, a very bumpy ride. Then got to walk around the Sphinx, and to enter into one of those huge pyramids and see where one of the Egyptian Kings was buried. The stone blocks used to build the pyramids were so large and heavy, one wonders how they got them stacked on top of the other. Is this what the Children of Israel were forced to build?

After sailing through the Suez Canal, we sailed down the Red Sea. I would stand at the ship's railing and look both ways across the sea. There was no place as we sailed along that I could see either side of the sea. I had to wonder how God made the water back up so the Children of Israel could walk through on dry ground when they left the land of Egypt.

I carried a picture of Deloris along with me, always having it setting on a dresser. The other guys would tease me constantly, and often her picture would be turned around backward, or would come up missing altogether, with no one having "any idea" what had happened to it. After a search of the room, it would be found in a drawer or closet somewhere.

Vietnam

Finally, on September 29, 1958, we arrived in Saigon, Vietnam, having traveled exactly one full month. How wonderful to be on solid ground again at last. On September 5, we arrived at our intended place of service at the Leprosarium hospital compound near the town of Ban Mê Thuột.

Don Voth, Corn, Oklahoma
Leland Good, Fisher, Illinois
Alan Hochstetler, Nappanee, Indiana

Letters we wrote to each other took five-to-seven days to be delivered. At one point, Deloris sent me a "care" package. It took six weeks to arrive. In her letter written October 5, 1958, Deloris talked about hula hoops. My question for her was, "What's a hula hoop?" Two months later, hula hoops arrived for sale in Saigon.

We had two kinds of pets in the house. We had a pair of beautiful parakeets. They had a green head and back, blue under the wings, a red tail, and a yellow beak. The other pet was a small civet cat with a spotted coat like a leopard. A native came by the house one day carrying this little kitten in his pocket. I bought it from him and gave him the name of Pogo. Pogo grew to the size of a large house cat, but had the temperament of a wild animal. In the evening he would lie on my lap and sleep while I was reading. Then without warning, he would dig his claws into my leg and take off running to another room. When he became a full grown cat, he would walk out into the jungle, but return by evening. As time went along, he was gone longer each time, until one day he just never returned. Most likely he realized he wasn't really a pet. Besides, he likely found himself a girlfriend.

One evening we saw something sail from one tree to another. It turned out to be a flying squirrel. It measured forty-two inches from its nose to the tip of its tail, with a wingspan of thirty-three inches. It basically spread out its front and back legs, and its skin formed a sort of kite, which it used to sail from one point to another. Its dark brown fur was super soft and silky to touch.

` Hunting

One of the Mennonite fellas had an Ithaca 12-gauge shotgun which he sold to me when he returned to The States. Since there were all kinds of animals in the jungle covering the mountains where we lived, I spent many hours hunting. During the day, while driving along the jungle roads leading to another village, I often sat on the hood of the Land Rover, holding the gun, because we often saw birds and animals on the road. There were wild chickens, like bantam chickens, and a beautiful black pheasant, much like our ring-necked pheasant. Sometimes on the road we would see peafowl that grew to the size of a turkey. Not only were they beautiful, especially if they were strutting with their tail fanned out, but they actually tasted better than domestic turkeys taste today.

Other animals in the jungle included all sorts of monkeys, wild hogs, wild cows, wild buffalo, wild elephants, and a huge buffalo-type animal known as a gaur.   There were also deer of all sizes. Some were the size of our mule and white tail deer. There was one the size of a large calf called a barking deer. Whenever it was frightened, it would bark similar to a dog's bark. When he stopped barking, you knew exactly where he would be standing. The most unusual and most beautiful deer was the mouse deer. It was a miniature deer about the size of a beagle dog. Its head was shaped like any deer, and its little feet were the size of my little finger, with cloven hooves, just like a large deer. Can you just imagine what fun God had creating all the different creatures?

To hunt at night, I would wear a spotlight on my head, something like a coal miner's light. Because I carried the gun, I would be the first one to walk down the path with the light. Behind me would be several tribesmen carrying little hatchets on their shoulders. They knew where the paths went through the jungle, and also knew what kind of animals we met as we were walking along. When the light shown on an animal, its eyes would reflect the light.   You could usually tell what kind of animal it was because the deer family have bright blue eyes, and the cat family (leopard and tiger) have red eyes. The most uncomfortable place to be in the hunting party is the last person in line.   Leopard cats sometimes would step off the path as the hunting party walked past, then would come up from behind and attack the last person in line. Sometimes we would ride in a basket on an elephant's back to hunt.

One time the tribesmen took several of us Americans hunting out on a large grassy area on the other side of the river. Crossing the river was an experience to start with. They had made a long raft by tying bamboo poles together. While I was crossing the river with most of the supplies, the raft got caught in the rapids in the middle of the river, and nearly upset. I was able to save our guns and supplies from falling into the river by grabbing hold of the raft with one hand, and grabbing hold of the supplies with the other.

The flat grassland had very few small trees, but was covered in places with heavy tall grass, about twelve feet tall. In the tall grass were paths the animals used to walk and hide in, with grass over the top so you couldn't see in or out. We walked through these paths at night, wondering what might be around the next corner.

Part of the land was covered in regular grass that the animals ate. Once, as I walked along shining my light around, I saw two of the largest blue eyes I have ever seen. They appeared to be twelve-to-sixteen inches apart. The tribesman behind me told me it was a gaur -- a huge, buffalo-type animal with a large set of horns, perhaps five feet wide. A large bull can easily weigh up to 2000 lbs., and have a very bad temperament. The animal has gristle that holds the horns in place. The correct place to shoot it is between the eyes. However, if you shoot a little above the eyes into the gristle, you will have one angry bull that will do his best to eliminate you, the hunter. Knowing all this, and considering the fact there were no trees to hide behind or climb, the size of my rifle (just a 30-06), and me being the only one having a gun, I walked as near to him as I could without scaring him away. I took careful aim, and was just ready to squeeze the trigger, when he lowered his huge head, and ran away. As he ran, the ground shook as if a freight train were going past.

Another night in another part of the country, we were hunting, while riding in a jeep. We were driving over the little hills shinning our lights around looking for game. We went over a little hill, only to find ourselves flying through the air, and landing in the river, jeep and all. What a surprise!

15

One time we were hunting in known tiger country. We set up camp at the bottom of a small hill, beside a small creek. We had a camp fire, but the other fellas thought we would sleep better with the fire light out. I thought the fire burning while we slept would keep the tiger away. I slept all night with my hand on my rifle, just in case. In the morning we went to the top of the little hill, and found tiger tracks in the sand where it had walked past us during the night.

Tigers were an animal to be respected. One day a man who lived forty-five miles away was killed by a tiger. Tribe's people lived in houses built up on stilts for protection, but we heard several stories where men walked out on the porch at night to relieve themselves, only to have a tiger jump up on the porch and kill the man. One night a tiger killed some cows in a village near the leprosarium. One of the cows belonged to one of the nurses that worked for us. The next night, he and I sat in a tree stand near the dead cow waiting for the tiger to return to eat again. There was a cool breeze blowing, and we got cold, so went home about 9:30 p.m. I wanted to go back out about midnight, but my bed was so inviting, I stayed home. The next morning we found the tiger had returned to eat again, sometime in the early morning hours.

One evening everyone was too busy to go hunting with me. Still I wanted to go, so I decided to just walk up the road a little. There was a path just off the road, about a quarter mile from the house. A hundred feet or so down the path, I saw a set of red eyes, less than fifteen feet away, looking at me. It took just a minute to realize it was a leopard, and I was all alone. Panic set in and I raised my gun and shot, then waited and listened, but heard nothing. Thinking I had killed the leopard, I went crashing into the jungle to look. I found nothing where the leopard had been standing seconds before. I quickly realized I must have fired into the air, and now was not just the hunter, but possibly the hunted as well. I hurried down the road, all the time shining the light into the jungle around me so as not to be attacked from behind or either side.

Another night while hunting with some natives, the guide showed me how to call the barking deer with a blade of grass held between my fingers. We walked to an area where we had seen some deer once before. I took the blade of grass, held it in my fingers and up to my mouth, blowing two puffs of air. Almost immediately, a barking deer came running up to us, and I shot it. We got two deer that night.

One more story! One of the International Voluntary Service fellas and I went hunting with a jeep. We drove several hours from our house to an area of rice patties. Rice patties are flat areas maybe fifty feet square, with a mound of dirt all the way around the patty. The mound is maybe sixteen inches high, and wide enough to walk on when the patties were filled with rice plants that grow in water. They were dry that night because it was the wrong season to grow rice. We had hunted all night and had seen nothing. It was about 3:00 a.m. when we saw some red eyes out in a patty. The animal would look at us, then lower his head behind a mound, then look at us again. My buddy decided it must be a small cat-type animal. He decided to carry his elephant rifle with him, but to use his pistol to shoot the animal. I was to stay on the jeep and hold the spotlight, so he could see the animal. He walked very close to the animal, and shot with his pistol. To our surprise, a full-grown leopard jumped up and attacked my buddy. The leopard's head and front paws reached as high as my buddies head, and his long tail dragged on the ground. All the while it growled, and snarled, preparing to tear my buddy apart. My buddy threw the pistol down, held his rifle in front of himself as some sort of protection, and quickly sidestepped. The leopard sailed past my buddy, not even touching him. The spotlight sort of blinded the leopard, and it then ran toward me and the jeep, then turned and ran into the darkness. I thought my buddy probably was dead, until I heard him shout, "Shoot him, shoot him!" My buddy walked up to the jeep, assuring me he didn't have a scratch. We shown the light all around the jeep and all over the fields of patties, but never seen the leopard again. We both lay down on the road and laughed ourselves silly.

I thoroughly enjoyed my hunting experiences and often provided fresh meat for the people who lived and worked at the leprosarium.

Leprosarium

The intended reason for our work at the leprosarium was to build a men's and women's ward on the hospital. Alan Hostetler, who grew up in Nappanee, Indiana, was selected as the contractor to draw up plans and oversee the building. He also was eighteen years old, and had worked construction with his father prior to this time, so he qualified as "the contractor."

The hospital had an old French Citroen truck, which we drove back through the jungle roads to the river. The road to the river was worse than a "good' cow path. It had huge stones, deep ruts cut by heavy rainfall, and huge tree roots to drive around or over. At the river we would shovel sand by hand onto the truck to haul back to the hospital to use in making cement blocks. We used a machine with a form shaped like a cement block. Sand was mixed with cement, then packed into the form. The machine then vibrated the sand into the shape of a block, after which the block was set aside to dry. These were made one at a time, over many weeks, by two native fellas we hired to help us.

Alan hired some Vietnamese wood cutters to get wood from the jungle to make lumber for the buildings. They found and cut down a tree with hard wood that was termite-proof. That tree measured about six foot in diameter at the base, and stood approximately 150 ft. tall. The one tree had enough wood to build the doors, windows, beds, and roof trusses for both buildings. All the lumber was cut with hand-powered, two-man saws. They cut 10" x 10" posts that were used for the porch posts to hold up the roof. They also cut some of the wood into boards measuring about ¾" x 25" x 10 ft. long, cut perfect shape and consistent size, all by a two-man hand saw.

Alan also designed and oversaw building of the septic system and installed plumbing for running water. I knew if you touched two wires together the sparks would fly. I (with this advanced knowledge of electrical systems) was given the job of wiring the buildings, helping to make them very modern, way out in the jungle, ten to twelve miles from the nearest town. The compound had two Continental diesel-powered generators that supplied the electricity when needed. We usually had power from mid-afternoon (the time when surgery was scheduled) until 10:00 p.m. most days. Other than that, we used gas lanterns for light.

When we first arrived at the Leprosarium compound, we began to study the local tribal Raday language. Our teacher, H'Cheia, was a sweet, soft spoken young woman of the Raday tribe. Her husband, Y' Dun, was of the Jari tribe. He spoke five languages, including English. He was studying to be a medical doctor, and was studying Russian on the side. Many of the young people, of both the tribes and Vietnamese, spoke several languages. We supposed "smart" American fellas only spoke one language. The Raday language has twenty one letters, and eighteen vowels, with some sounds used to pronounce some of the words, that we were not used to. The other two fellas seemed to learn to speak fairly quickly, while I sort of lagged along behind. Over the three years of my work there, I was able to keep up with most all the conversation. It was very interesting to sit around a fire at night, and listen to the old men tell stories from when time began: the story about the "flood" as recorded in the Bible; why the white men have guns, and the Raday only have blowguns. These people were kind, gentle, and soft spoken. They treated us young Americans with much respect. When I would tell them to do

21

something, or give them some advice, they would answer, "Whatever you say, Grandfather." I was not used to being respected like that. After all, I was only eighteen years old. They were smaller in stature than we Americans, and had rich brown skin, likely of Malaysian origin. They quickly became close friends.

Several miles from the leprosarium was a mighty, huge waterfall. We often went there to swim and to have a picnic lunch. The river above the falls split, creating an island between the two river channels that plunged over the falls. One time the group decided to swim across the first channel to explore the island in the middle. I wasn't a real good swimmer. When I reached the middle of the channel where the water was moving fast, I began to be swept toward the falls. I yelled for help, and Alan jumped in and helped me across. Another time we were swimming in a quiet pool below the falls. I was climbing a rock wall, using the boulders to stand on and to pull myself up. One of the boulders I was using to pull myself up with, a stone of 18 - 20 inches, came loose and fell over my head and down behind me into the water. Needless to say, I followed the stone, falling down into the water below. I have an idea my guardian angel often said, "Oh no, look out, he's awake again." I am thankful for the many times the Lord, "watched over" me throughout my life time.

After the hospital was built, Alan was transferred to Nha Trang, a city on the ocean. He was to build a new MCC unit house and hospital right on one of the most beautiful beaches in Vietnam. We called it the "hardship post."

I stayed at the leprosarium to do maintenance for the remainder of my term. I did jobs like automobile maintenance, which was an unending job. The whole electrical system needed updating, including replacing the old poles and cross arms and stringing new wires.

We had been pumping the water we needed from a stream that the village upstream used to wash clothes and bathe in as well. The water was filtered through a clay-type filter before we drank it. We were able to hire an American company that was drilling wells throughout Vietnam to come drill a well of pure water for our use. We put a large square steel drum up on the side of the mountain to us as a water reservoir. To get the drum up on the mountain, we used the winch that was on the front of the old Dodge Power Wagon. We ran the cable up the mountain, around a tree, and back down to the drum. Then we wound the cable back onto the winch, pulling the drum up to the place we had prepared for the drum to sit. The water was pumped up to the drum each day, using a small gasoline engine attached to the pump. We now had plenty of pure water, and more than enough water pressure. Some of the old existing water lines burst from the pressure and had to be replaced.

As a side story, after Deloris and I had been married thirty-some years, we began attending the Archbold Evangelical Mennonite Church in Archbold, Ohio. One of the members of the church was a man by the name Pat Frey, a well driller. When I showed him the picture from when we were drilling the well in Vietnam, he told me the man doing the drilling was his nephew.

Alan Hochstetler and I bought a German-built motorcycle. Its top speed reached about 60 mph. We rode that bike many miles around that county.

23

One day I was driving on the main paved road, in the mountains, at top speed to be sure. As I approached a dozen or so tribe's people walking along the road, the group separated, and stood on both sides of the road to let me pass by. As I came close to the group, a little girl decided to quickly cross to the other side of the road. I began to slow down and apply the brake, intending to pass behind her. However, the little girl turned around again and ran back to the side she had been on to start with. Now I am in real trouble. I pretty much laid the bike on its side, sliding very close behind her, but not hitting her. I then was able to get the bike to right itself back up, only to have it lay down on the opposite side. Once more the bike came back upright, and I was able to gain control of it. I glanced back to be sure they were indeed alright, then continued riding away as quickly as possible. I would have liked to stop and apologize for frightening them, but at the same time I didn't know for sure if they were friendly or not. This is another time I give praise to the Lord for protecting me from serious injury, or possible death.

In November of 1959, I got sick. My weight went from 150 to 139 lbs. I was so sick they discussed the idea of sending me home, because they could not figure out what was wrong. I did not want to be sent home. I was sent to the hospital in Saigon, where they discovered I had Amoebic Dysentery, and Hook worm. With the proper treatment and medication, I recovered and was able to complete my term of service.

During the school year of 1959, Deloris studied secretarial training and graduated from Goshen College. We wrote at least one letter each week. Each air mail letter she sent me cost her .25 cents. She told me that her second semester books cost $6.31. I wanted to send her a skirt woven by the tribe's ladies, so asked her for her waist size. Several weeks later she replied, half apologizing, she told me her waist measured 26 inches. She was always able to keep her slender look throughout her entire life.

Viet Cong

In late 1959 / early 1960, we began to become aware of Viet Cong activity in the surrounding villages, from time to time. We were, for the most part, able to continue traveling and working like usual.

One evening a car load of us Americans were going into town, probably for Bible study / prayer meeting. Several miles from the Leprosarium, we met several armed men, dressed in black standing in the road. We stopped. They ask us where we were going, and where we were from. We knew without being told they were members of the Viet Cong. After talking to us a few minutes, they disappeared into the jungle as quickly as they had appeared.

As we were returning from a full day medical clinic in a village out in the countryside, I was driving the Land Rover. We were driving on a sandy dirt road, lined with small trees and brush. Because the dust was coming into the back of the Rover, I stopped and walked around back to tie down the canvas cover. I nearly had it tied down, when someone fired a shot. I instantly heard the bullet whistle right over my head. I quickly stepped on the other side of the Rover, jumped in and had one of the other staff move into the drivers seat and drive quickly away. I am thankful that person was a poor shot, or else maybe he just wanted to frighten us away.

Later in 1960 and 1961, Viet Cong activity began to increase. We had one of the national workers who seemed to know each morning where the activity had been during the night.

I lived by myself in a small wooden house near one end of the hospital compound, close up against the jungle. Late one evening, there was an urgent knock on my door, and someone speaking in Raday said, "Open the door! It's the Viet Cong! We've come to take you away!" I told them to give me a couple of minutes and I will open the door. Actually, I was trying to buy some time, trying to decide what to do. I considered running out the back door into the jungle to see if I could escape. However, I assumed the house was surrounded, and if I tried to run, I would get shot. They again pounded on the door and said, "Open up! We've come to take you away!" After stalling as long as I thought I dared, I opened the door. There stood the national worker we suspected knew the movements of Viet Cong. He burst out laughing and said, "I really scared you, didn't I." I told him I didn't think that was very funny.

One night the Viet Cong came and burned the bridge on the road, near the end of our driveway, cutting off travel on the road between the hospital and the town. They had hung a picture of the President of the country on a post. They had put holes in the picture where his eyes were, and had cut his throat.

The next day was Sunday, and all seemed quiet. About mid-afternoon I heard army trucks coming and stopping down by the bridge. I decided to check out what was happening, so I walked down the little path toward the out-patient clinic. Nearing the clinic, I noticed soldiers behind every tree, and each one had his rifle pointed at me. Not a good feeling. Soon about six soldiers came walking around the clinic, walking toward me. The commander in charge gave a signal, and all the soldiers lowered their guns and came out from behind the trees. The commander spoke to me in Vietnamese. I said, "I don't speak Vietnamese." He then spoke to me in French. I said, "I don't speak French." Then he said in English, "Are you an American?" I said yes. He asked me, "Aren't you afraid?" I told him no. He asked me, "Have you seen any Viet Cong?" They then spread out in a long line and searched the compound, looking under buildings and all around, looking for the enemy.

Mountain People

I enjoyed my work with the mountain people, and became good friends with many of them. Following are some stories of my work with these wonderful people.

When I first arrived at the hospital, a village woman gave birth to twins. Because of evil spirit worship and control, it was considered a curse to give birth to twins. Normally the babies were taken out into the jungle and laid just off the path to die, or to be eaten by wild animals. We Christian workers from the hospital went to the village and were able to convince the chief of the village, that twins were a double blessing, and not a curse. We were successful in changing a long standing tradition and saving the babies' lives.

The people would walk many miles to bring a sick person from their village to the clinic we had on the hospital compound. One of the Nationals, a tribesman and a pastor, came to be admitted to the clinic hospital. He had what they called Black Water Fever. He was very sick for a number of weeks -- so sick, in fact, that he just lay there like dead, not communicating in any way. One afternoon, the missionary mechanic, Bob McNeel, told me the missionaries were going to the hospital to pray for this man. He asked, "Do you want to go along?" I said, "Oh no, I am not a missionary, I'm just a common man, a mechanic." He asked, "You are a believer in Jesus Christ, aren't you?" I answered, "Oh yes," and he replied, "Then you can come along too, if you want to." I really wanted to go along with them, so with his encouragement, I went along.

At the hospital we all stood around the bed of the sick man. Someone read a portion of scripture, then they anointed him with oil, according to the instruction in the Bible. All the men put their hands on the sick man. When I hesitated, they encouraged me to put my hand on him too. After a short prayer for healing, the leader called the man by name. Instantly, the sick man turned his head and looked at the leader. A week or so later that man walked out of the hospital and returned to his village, a healed man.

Another time there was a man who came to the hospital for treatment. We soon realized his sickness was not physical, but spiritual. The doctor decided I should take the man back to his village, as we could not care for him, and he was disrupting the work at the clinic. As I was talking to the man about going home, I looked into his eyes, and instantly saw the eyes of a demon possessed man. I will never forget that wild look. I wish I had known we as Christians have authority over evil spirits.

Lots of the tribe's people came in to the hospital to deliver their babies. One evening they delivered a baby that had been dead for some time already. After delivery, the nurse called me, and gave me the child, wrapped in a cloth, and told me to go bury it somewhere. I dug a hole out in the yard, under a large tree, not far from the hospital. Then I laid the little child in the hole, and covered it up, just like you would bury a cat or dog. I will never forget that task, and how I felt.

Another time a very pregnant lady was walking from her village to our hospital to give birth to her child. Several miles from the hospital, the baby decided it was time to be born. The lady squatted beside the road and gave birth to the child. She wrapped the child in a dirty blanket, and continued the walk to the hospital. Both mother and baby were in excellent health on arrival at the hospital. The tribe's people were physically very strong -- much more so than the average American.

One afternoon, a hospital patient from a distant village died. Don Voth and I loaded the body and several of the family into the back of the International Carryall, to take them back to the village, maybe thirty miles away. We approached the village after 10:00 p.m., and the people in the village had already started to wail before we arrived. I have no idea how they knew about the death before we arrived.

Sometime around midnight, we started our journey back to the hospital. The road here was just a dirt path in the jungle, wide enough to drive through. About a half mile from the village, we drove down a rather steep hill. At the bottom, the van tipped to one side as the one front wheel broke and fell off. We knew there was a little church in the village several miles up the road, so decided to walk there to spend the remainder of the night. Not having a light of any kind, we walked in the dark, praying for protection from wild animals or any other danger along the way. The pastor let us sleep on the floor of the little church, and in the morning, he let us use his little motorbike to ride back to the hospital. Needless to say, our coworkers were really concerned, as we had not returned all night. After a search in the little town of Ban Mê Thuột, we found a two-wheeled trailer-like thing we could pull behind our old Dodge Power Wagon. It had a crank up arm that we were able to put under the front of the broken vehicle, and lift it off the ground. That was all fine, except the road was muddy and we couldn't get traction to move the load up the hill. The power wagon was equipped with a cable and winch on the front. We ran the cable out and hooked it to a tree up on the hill. Using the winch, and the four wheel drive, we were able to get the vehicles up to the top of the hill, and then on home. A mechanic in Ban Mê Thuột was able to weld the wheel back on good enough we could drive the International. Many months later, the new parts arrived from the U.S. so we could fix the vehicle correctly.

One day I went down to the men's ward at the hospital to visit with the men. One man was looking at a National Geographic magazine. Some time in my life prior to this, I read (also in National Geographic) of a tribesman looking at the pictures in a magazine, with the magazine upside down. You can guess my surprise to find one of these men looking at the pictures upside down. I took the magazine from him, turned it right side up and said, "That's a really good picture of ..." whatever it was. He took the magazine back, turned it upside down again, looked at it again and said, "Yes, that sure is." I have no idea what was going on in his head.

One of the men who had leprosy, and lived in one of the houses provided for patients with leprosy, had a pet Maya bird. I went to visit him and ask him, "Where is your bird?" He replied, "It is out walking in the jungle, but it will come home if I call him." He called the bird's name out the window several times. We could hear the bird squawking somewhere out in the jungle, and in a few minutes, the bird flew in the window and sat on his shoulder.

When Alan moved to NhaTrang to begin construction of a MCC unit house there, I hauled some of the building material with our old French truck across the mountains, down to the coast where the new unit was located. Near the halfway point, and just before driving through the mountains, was a place to rest a bit, and a little restaurant to get something to eat or drink. I had stopped for something to drink, and was sitting alone at one of the tables. In another corner of the restaurant there were eight-to-ten tribe's men, sitting there visiting and talking. They were talking about the "American" truck driver. They knew all about me, where I was from in the country, and what we Americans were doing for them at the leprosarium. After some time, one of them, again talking about me, said, "But he doesn't understand our language." I quickly answered them, just as they would have answered, "Why wouldn't I understand your language?" They looked at me in disbelief, then jumped up from the table and said, "He does understand us and he knows all we have been saying about him." We all had a good laugh together.

Once when I went to a village to pick up a sick lady to bring her to the hospital, a man in the village put corn husks on the lady's head to protect her from the evil spirits.

One Sunday I attended the little church just across the road from the leprosarium compound. It had benches to sit on, but didn't have any back rests. The benches got plenty hard until the service was over. It was fun to sing hymns that we sing here in America, only in their native language. It was the Sunday they had the communion service. We were served bread as usual, but for wine, they served orange Kool-Aid.

When Alan moved to Nha Trang to work, I was put in charge of the work, and the employees at the hospital. This elevated me to a new level of respect. Some of the workers and other people removed their hats when I passed in the car. Some would even bow before they would talk to me. This was difficult for me. I wanted to say, "Hey people, I'm just a common country boy."

Once I went with Olive Kingsbury, one of the nurses to a segregated village, a village of leprous people. The chief of the village told us, "No one ever comes to visit us except the tigers." In the evening, Olive told them the Bible story of Jonah, who was thrown into the ocean and swallowed by a big fish. One of the natives asked, "Why didn't he kill the fish with his axe?" Every tribesman always carries a little axe on his shoulder, much like many of us men carry a knife in our pocket.

The leprosarium was located out in the jungle, about eight miles from the small town of Ban Mê Thuột. On a good day, you could drive to town in about twenty minutes. During the rainy season, it took closer to forty-five minutes. One section of the road, maybe ¼ mile long, ran through a swampy area. This part of the road was full of large holes that would be full of water, and the mud was as slippery as a greased pig. Some of the holes were five-to-six feet wide and maybe one-and-a-half feet deep. To drive through this part of the road during the rainy season, you basically put the jeep or truck into first gear, then slowly eased yourself into and out of one hole into another hole. If you had any little children riding with you, they always went to sleep in that quarter mile because of the rocking motion of the vehicle.

The leprosarium had a Ford tractor that was equipped with a blade on the front. During the dry season, we pushed dirt from the side of the road into the large holes in the road to make the road easier to travel on. The next rainy season, the dirt turned to mud, and got pushed out, and the holes appeared again.

Then came the day in the fall of 1961 when it was time for me to leave Vietnam, and return to the U.S. It was both a sad day, and a day of excitement. The tribe's people came to my house one afternoon, to have a "visit," or a farewell for Don and me. They said nice things about us and our work for them. They also played musical instruments and sang songs for us. They gave us gifts of small dishes of uncooked rice, and some small gift items. If you had been a really important person, they would put an egg in the rice in the center of the bowl.

I remember watching out of the window of the airplane as we flew over the little town of Ban Mê Thuột, and then over the leprosarium and the beautiful jungle that had been "home" for three wonderful years.

The Trip Home

Don and I flew from Saigon to Hong Kong on the first leg of our trip home. We stayed with some fellas that were working there with MCC. They took us to a small British protectorate connected to China, called Macau. We rented bicycles and rode all around the country. The road goes to a low stone wall, or fence which divides the country between Macau and Communist China. The Chinese people can cross over to Macau to trade at the city, then ride the bus back into China. We rode our bikes up to the wall where there was a young soldier with a rifle. He said to us, "You need to stop, or I will have to shoot you." He was about our age, so we visited with him for quite a while, using several languages including English, French, and Cantonese, as I remember. While eating in a Café, we saw a lady missionary to China, Gladys Alyward. A book, *The Small Woman*, written by Alan Burgess, tells the story of her life.

Next we flew to Japan where we spent several days sightseeing and visiting Mennonite missionaries in Tokyo. While there, we visited the Nortake china factory, where I picked out a beautiful twelve-piece set of china to take home for my girlfriend, who I hoped to marry. Interesting to me now that I didn't consult her about her likes or dislikes in the matter. At Christmas I gave it to her as a Christmas / engagement present. She liked it very much, and we enjoyed using it during our married years, whenever guests stopped to visit us.

We booked passage on a Norwegian freighter, named the S. S. Turandot to sail across the Pacific Ocean to Los Angeles, California. If I remember right, it took two weeks to sail across the ocean. Being a freighter, there were only about a dozen passengers on board. Among the passengers I remember were Mr. and Mrs. Miller, a very well-to-do couple, from Tucson, Arizona, and a middle-aged couple from St. Petersburg, Florida, who were just married, and on their honeymoon trip around the world. I also remember an eighty-year-old Grandma, who was sailing around the world, "To use up her money, so her kids wouldn't get any of it." And of course, we two country boys -- Don Voth and me.

It was an interesting trip. We ate all our meals at the captain's table, and were given a tour down inside the ship to see the engine and how it worked. It was huge, the size of a semi trailer. It had six cylinders which were twenty four inches in diameter. Each piston had a stroke, or moved, ten-and-a-half-foot, and weighed four tons each. The ship's speed was twenty one mph.

Eating with the captain was very interesting and informative. However, during dinner one evening, Mr. Miller began telling stories about horse racing. The captain soon asked him to stop talking about horses. Mr. Miller laughed it off, and continued. Shortly, the captain raised his voice, and told Mr. Miller to stop talking about horses, because that would cause a storm on the ocean before morning. Mr. Miller just laughed, but stopped talking about horses.

When we awoke the next morning, the ship was tossing like a cork on the angry sea. The waves were so large, some of them splashed over the front of the ship. It was frightening.

Due to the rocking and tossing of the ship, the servers took action to keep the dishes from slipping off the breakfast tables. They raised the edges of the tables, and put four or five layers of table cloth down, then poured water on them. We had just been served our food, when the ship was pushed to one side by a huge wave, then immediately pushed back the other way, causing all the dishes and food to slide off the table and crash on to the floor. I flew off of my chair, and landed in the lap of the grandma. It sounded like the ship might have broken in half.

The dining staff helped clean up the mess, and then brought new dishes and food to the table and we again began to eat breakfast. About half way through the meal, the captain appeared, and stood in the doorway, just looking at Mr. Miller. After a while he spoke, "Mr. Miller, what did I tell you?" He was not a very happy man.

34

One morning when we woke up, the ship's engine was not running. The rings on one of the pistons had broken and had to be replaced. We drifted all day as the mechanics replaced the piston and got the engine running again. The newly wed couple wanted to go fishing, but we didn't have a fish hook. We managed to find some string, and tried bending a pin into the shape of a hook. Needless to say, we didn't catch anything.

On the last night of the voyage, the captain threw a party. The captain gave Don and me Coke to drink, while everyone else had plenty of alcohol. The wife of the newly wed couple had way too much to drink, so her husband took her to their room and put her to bed, then came back to the party. Some time later he went to their room to check on her. He soon returned and said she was no longer in their room, and he couldn't find her anywhere.

The captain told everyone to search the ship for her, and he slowed the ship so it could be turned around. They turned on the search lights and began to search the waves in case she had fallen overboard. Don and I hunted all over the deck and finally found her, in a dark corner, curled up under some deck chairs, asleep. She apparently tried to find her way back to the party but got lost. When everything was again under control, Don and I were talking with the captain. Most people from other countries drink alcohol like we drink coffee. He said, "Damned Americans, they don't know when to stop." Because of that incident and having to stop the ship, we were a day late getting into the Los Angeles port.

Home Again, At Last

I knew my parents and my younger brother, Loren, were going to meet the ship at the port in Los Angeles. They were supposed to bring my girlfriend Deloris along. As they docked the ship, Don and I stood at the railing on the deck, watching, and looking to see if our families had come to meet us. The ship's deck was thirty feet or so above the level of the dock. Finally I saw four people approaching the ship. I recognized my Mom and Dad, and my girl friend, Deloris, but couldn't figure who the big guy was, standing with Deloris. After some time, I began to realize the big guy was my little brother, who had grown up while I was away. How exciting to be reunited with family for the first time in three years.

It didn't take Deloris and me long to decide we wanted to get married. When I told my parents of our engagement, Papa said, "Already?" At first I worked for Jasper Roth, my brother-in-law, in farming and carpentry, for $1.25 per hour. My buddy, Bud Swartzentruber, drove gas tanker truck, and said I could drive for the same company for $2.50 - $2.90 per hour. What would I do with that much money?

In the spring of 1962, I started working for Sauder Manufacturing, in Archbold, Ohio. I took a room in a home owned by an old Mennonite lady who rented rooms to men from other communities. It seems to me that over the years, she had forty-plus renters.

A Husband and Father

Deloris and I were married June 30, 1962. We rented a big old farm house in the country, for which we paid $10.00 rent per month. We loved the old house in the summer time and made a huge garden. Winter was another story. The house had two oil space heaters which could hardly keep the house warm. One Sunday afternoon we were sitting in the living/dining room visiting. The outside basement door blew open, and the linoleum covering the dining room floor, floated up about two feet above the floor because of the wind blowing into the basement doorway. A year later, Timothy Leland was born. The next year, after his birth, we rented another large farm house nearer to Deloris' parents. Not caring for factory work, I took a job working for Uncle Vernon Graber doing carpentry work. When we had work, we worked, when we had no work, we didn't work.

I soon found work with Hit Archery, making archery equipment, and trophies. My job was to shape the handle section of the bow with the end of a belt sander. I prided myself with having the ability to shape each bow exactly like the one before. Sometimes a customer wanted the handle of his bow "custom-made." I enjoyed being able to make his handle "just right."

In 1968, a second boy, Keith Ryan, was born, followed five years later by a little girl, Miriam Sue.

After working for Hit Archery for several years, I got work with Lugbill Supply, a building supply store in Archbold, Oh. I worked there as head of the paint department, and head sales clerk. I worked for them for twenty-three years. Many times, customers would stand in line, waiting for me to help them with their purchases. That helped my self-worth grow. I made many friends over the years working there. When our family would walk downtown, many people would greet us, calling me by name. Our children often asked, "Does everyone know who you are?"

During the time I worked at Lugbill Supply, I got overcome with lawn and garden insecticide. The poison made my body react like a bug reacts when he is dying from being sprayed. The EMTs were called and they gave me an injection which neutralized the poison, but I was sick for many weeks. If I would become nervous, my body would shake like I was cold, until my teeth would chatter. Also I developed severe hypoglycemia. Several years later, being almost too tired to work, I started taking Chelation -- an I.V. treatment, made up of several medications, which washed much of the poison out of my blood. Within two weeks of beginning this treatment, I began to feel improvement. Over the years, taking many I.V. treatments, my health is fairly normal.

While working at Lugbills, Owens Corning Fiberglass Company ran a contest for the customers. The prize was an all-expense paid trip to one of four sports events. The sales person put his name on an entry blank, then gave the customer the entry blank to sign and send in. If the customer won the trip, the sales person got to go along on the trip. Imagine my surprise, when one of my customers won the prize. Deloris and I, and my customer and his friend went to the World Cup Down Hill Ski event in Aspen, Colorado. It was late winter / early spring, and cold. We stayed in a nice motel in Aspen. We enjoyed the pool and the hot tub in spite of the fact there was three feet of snow on the sidewalk around the pool. It was fun sitting in the hot tub in the night, while big snow flakes fell all around us.

When we married, we decided we would save some money each year for a trip to Hawaii to celebrate our twenty-fifth wedding anniversary. What a wonderful vacation we had, enjoying the sun and the water. Deloris wasn't too comfortable in the water. However, she consented to go snorkeling with a group. She enjoyed it so much, we later borrowed equipment from a friend, and went by ourselves the second time. That time we saw little blue and yellow, and multi colored fish that came up and ate out of our hands. One interesting fish was maybe eighteen inches long, and shaped like a pencil. It would swim through the water, like a snake crawls on the ground. It liked eating the frozen peas we fed it from our hand.

The first church we attended was Inlet Mennonite Church. Driving there took nearly a half hour, and then the same time back home again. We drove there two times on Sunday, Wednesday evening, and then any special meetings during the week. We began to realize it would be much better to live in that area, near the church, rather than drive from a distance. We purchased a twenty-acre farm with a house and barn, just a half mile north of the church.

We paid $13,500.00 for the property, and were able to get a thirty-year loan. A few years later, we built an addition on the west end of the house. The addition consisted of a kitchen/dining area, new wash room, and one upstairs bedroom.

A Pilot

As a boy growing up, I always watched the pigeons fly from building to building on the farm. I decided I wanted to fly too, someday. The second year of our marriage, I began to take flying lessons at the local airport, and earned my private license. It was lots of fun taking the family up for a ride on a Sunday afternoon or evening. Keith was a little boy. Almost as soon as we were in the air, he would go to sleep, and sleep until we would touch down again. Nearly always he would say, "That was a really nice ride."

One winter weekend we flew to visit my family in Illinois. The trip out was uneventful, other than arriving late in the afternoon. We had to find a pay phone to call my brother to come pick us up. The airport manager always told us to plan our trip so as to arrive back at the airport with just a little fuel left in the airplane. He said the gas at the airport was lots cheaper than we could purchase at another location, so plan to come back nearly empty. He wanted to fill the airplane with fuel from the pumps at the home airport. We arrived at the airport in Illinois with both tanks of the airplane half full of fuel. I told Deloris, "Look, we have just the right amount of fuel to fly home again."

The day we returned to Ohio was sunny with small puffy white clouds. As we flew along, the clouds began to thicken, and before we realized it, we could no longer see the ground. We were following the radio that told us we were going the right direction, but we could no longer tell exactly where we were. Besides that, both gas gauges were showing both fuel tanks were empty. Still we could not see the ground. I tried calling for help on the radio, thinking we must surely be near Fort Wayne, Indiana, unaware I was using old, discontinued radio call numbers. We began to pray for wisdom and for help. We began to see small holes in the cloud cover beneath us. Although I knew it was illegal, I told Deloris as soon as I see a hole the size of the airplane, we were going to drop through the clouds so we could at least see where we could attempt to land if the engine stopped. Shortly we found a hole and dropped through the clouds, finding ourselves near the ground, flying in a snow storm. A look at the map and the ground told me we had about fifteen minutes to the airport at Auburn, Indiana. I have no doubt in my mind, God kept the airplane engine running on fumes until we landed and bought some fuel. Back in the air, we headed for Wauseon, arriving at our airport after dark. I had never flown at night, but as we arrived at the airport, the snow covered landing strip stood out like a cement runway at noon, and we made a perfect landing and taxied up to our waiting car in total darkness, safe and sound.

A Man After God

Living near the church allowed us to get acquainted with the people who lived in the neighborhood. The plan was to be able to invite them to become involved in the church. We joined in the work of the church, teaching class, leading singing, printing bulletins, cleaning the building, serving as elder, and as MYF sponsor. We enjoyed being part of a growing church family.

The work of the church was going well, but Deloris and I began to get hungry for more of a daily walk with the Lord. Surely there must be more to following Jesus than just going to church on Sunday, and working all week again, waiting for next Sunday. Besides that, there was this fella from Archbold, Bud Hitt, who I used to work for, who would stop in at the store and tell me stories about his daily walk with the Lord. He told me things like, "God told me to stop and talk with this man, and he accepted Jesus as his Savior." Or, "God told me to pray for this sick lady and she got healed." I would go home in the evening, and tell Deloris what Bud had said. We both wanted whatever he was talking about.

There were some meetings being held at the Archbold Evangelical Mennonite church over one weekend that focused on personal living, and husband-and-wife relationships, related to our walk with God. Deloris and I enjoyed the teaching we received during the meetings. One of the speakers urged us to give everything we have back to God as an offering of thanksgiving, and surrender to Him. It wasn't too hard to "give back" things, like cars, the farm, my job, and such things. But it was extremely hard, and frightening to give Him my wife, and my children.

Besides becoming involved in the local Full Gospel Business Men's organization, we began to have a daily time of Bible reading and prayer. One of us would read a portion of scripture, and the other one would lead in prayer. The next evening we would switch reading and praying. One evening when I began to pray, I experienced the presence of the Lord in an unusual way. When I told Deloris what had just happened, she told me that had happened to her the night before. She had not told me, because she was afraid of what I might think. We didn't know what it meant, but when I told my friend Bud about it, he just smiled, and told me we had just been touched by the Holy Spirit.

After being, "touched" by the Holy Spirit, the Bible began to read "different" than it had before. It was so interesting, I couldn't find enough time to read more of it. When we sang the hymns in church, the songs seemed to have "new meaning" and exciting words. We were really excited. However, when we tried to tell our church friends about what we experienced, many of them seemed offended, like something was wrong with us.

About this same time, there was a "new" church, meeting at the Stryker High School. We went to visit, and began to attend the Sunday evening service. Our children wanted to go there all the time, but we had responsibilities at our church we felt we needed to complete. At the end of the year, when these were completed, we began attending the Stryker church along with the children. We hated leaving our church friends behind, but enjoyed the singing and the teaching we received at the new church.

Our daughter, Miriam, graduated from Bluffton College with a teaching degree. She took a teaching position with the Living Word Christian School. One year while on a mission trip to Bogota, Colombia, she was invited to return there, to teach in their Christian School. She took that position as a teacher, and stayed two years. She invited her mother and me to come visit, which we did. The second year she met and became engaged to be married to Daniel Hernandez, a young man in the church she attended. She invited us to come visit again, to meet his family. Then because it was taking so long to get his "papers" to come to the U.S., they decided to get married there, and invited us to come the third time, for the wedding. We bought tickets, and made plans to go to the wedding. However, shortly before the planned wedding in Bogota, Dan received permission to come to our country. They jumped on a plane, while Deloris and I planned the wedding for them here.

Now, since we had purchased air tickets, and the wedding took place here, we had tickets to use and nowhere to go. That's when we discovered the island of Aruba. Aruba is an island south of the U.S., and not far from the coast of South America. It is approximately six miles wide and twenty miles long. It has beautiful beaches to enjoy during the day, and casinos to receive your money during the night. We spent a week there, enjoying the sunshine, and living in a beautiful condo. We even toured a "time share" that was for sale. We decided it was not a good idea to buy into it as a yearly vacation spot. What if we wanted to spend our yearly vacation somewhere else?

Change in Vocation

After working for Lugbill Supply for twenty-three years, I again became restless with the everyday routine, wishing for some other kind of work. I began to pray for a job that I would have some "desk work" along with some physical labor. In the newspaper was an advertisement for a sales position in real estate. I enrolled in the local community college, studying real estate sales. There were four required classes to pass the course, and here I was, already middle aged.   I told my wife, "I will take the classes one at a time.   As long as I pass the class, I will continue."   To my surprise, I got an "A" in each class.   When I took the required, State test, I passed it, "just squeaking through."   When I began selling real estate for Realty World, Short Agency, the manager told me, "You passed the test, now we will teach you how to sell real estate."   Again, doing this type of sales work for nearly eighteen years, I made lots of friends, and enjoyed helping young couples qualify for, and purchase, their "first" home. It was during this time we began buying old homes to fix up to rent, or sell. We bought and rebuilt eight homes in Wauseon.

Return to Vietnam

Throughout our married life, I always talked about, and told my wife and children, stories of my time of service in the country of Vietnam. Then in 2006, we joined a two-week tour to the country of Vietnam, lead by Tour Magination.   My sister, Dolorez Roth from Paxton, Illinois joined us.

A group of thirteen people left New York City airport just after dark, and flew to Anchorage, Alaska.   There they refueled the airplane, and an hour later we headed for a city in China. Because we were flying west, we flew in darkness for seventeen hours before arriving the next morning in daylight. Switching planes, we flew to Hanoi, North Vietnam. We stayed in beautiful, modern hotels, and had excellent food to eat. We visited museums, gardens, ancient rulers' palaces, and many places of interest. The tour took us south, stopping to visit various cities as we worked our way to Saigon, now known as Ho Chi Minh City.

One city we visited was Hội An, where we visited a small Mennonite church. They were actually meeting illegally, in the pastor's home. The pastor's wife served us a sort of rice cake wrapped in a banana leaf, and some coffee. The pastor spoke some English, so we were all able to understand the story he told of the church.   I gave him my real estate business card that had my picture on it. He said, "Oh, this is good. I wish I had pictures of everyone on the tour. That way I could remember to pray for each of you every day." Tears came to my eyes. Why should he be praying for me? Rather, I should be praying for him and his church.

We visited the city of Nha Trang, and stayed on the tenth floor of a new hotel, overlooking a beautiful beach. Deloris and I took time to go for a swim at the beach. During my years of working in the country, I had helped haul material to build a MCC unit house in this town. The house was situated within walking distance of another beautiful beach. We were able to visit the house and hospital that was staffed by MCC, and VNCS, Vietnam Christian Service personal, prior to and during the war. Many buildings and the surroundings had changed enough over the years, making it difficult to recognize the exact buildings.

While visiting the city of Saigon, we had dinner with one of the Mennonite pastors who had just been released after being in prison for four years. He and his young wife were excited about serving the Lord, and leading the church. He invited two couples with the tour to come have lunch at their home the next day. While they were there visiting, there was a knock at the door. There stood a policeman. The policeman said, "I understand you have foreigners in your home." The pastor invited him in and introduced him to his visitors. The one couple had been missionaries in Vietnam, while the other was a doctor, serving the people of Vietnam. After visiting about a half hour, the policeman stood and prepared to leave. He said, "I have just been doing my job."

The same time, my sister, and my wife and I went up country to visit the area where I had spent time working at the Leprosarium. We were given a map of the city, which had grown from several thousand, to a large city of 10,000 people. We stayed at a modern hotel with a nice pool out back. Ordering something to eat was a little difficult since I didn't speak Vietnamese, but what they served us was always good.

I knew several tribe's people who lived in the city, who I had worked with back in 1969. The one man's daughter lives in the United States, and had visited our home once. She told me to just go to the village and ask for "dad." He lived just across town, so we hailed a cab, to go visit him. The cab driver seemed nervous about our request, and talked to someone on his cell phone the whole trip. When we got near the area we had asked him to take us, he motioned for us to get out. We paid him the fee and he pointed in the direction we needed to walk to get to our destination.

We met a man who I asked in his tribal language if he knew Mr. Y' Dun. He took us to a small church, where the pastor was teaching English to young people. When he took us to Y' Dun's house, we waited outside while he went in to tell Y' Dun we had come to visit. Soon he came out and told us Y' Dun had gone away earlier that day. Next I ask about Y' Dun's brother in law, Mr. Y' Sieok. We went to his house and, after waiting outside like before, the pastor came back out and told us that Y' Sieok was sick and couldn't come to the door. As we prepared to walk away, Y' Seiok's wife stood in the doorway to see who had come to visit. I recognized her right away and spoke to her. She invited us into her home, asking us to sit on the sofa. I began showing her some pictures we had brought along, one picture being of her niece and husband, who live in the U.S., and who had visited in our home.

We had been in her home perhaps four minutes when someone took a hold of my shoulder. When I looked, here it was the police. He motioned to us that we needed to leave immediately. We walked out of the house and intended to walk away, but the officer motioned to us that we needed to stay with him. Presently the Police Paddy Wagon came, and we were loaded into the back seat for the trip to the Police Station. Arriving downtown at the "police station," they opened a big overhead door. Inside the building was a couch where they had us sit, several other chairs, and a table or two. We each began praying, as we were so thirsty, and so hot and afraid what might happen to us. One of the officers took my sister's camera away from her, and set it on a table across the room. Another officer came with three glasses and a bottle of water. My sister whispered, "Are we going to drink that water?" I told her, yes, we don't want to do anything to upset them. He poured water into one glass, swished it around, poured it into the second glass, swished it around, poured it into the third glass, swished it around, and dumped it out onto the floor. He then filled the glasses and gave each of us a glass of water to drink. At that point I thought to myself, maybe they won't be mean to us.

They arranged a table in the middle of the room, with five chairs on one side, and three on the other side, then asked us to come sit at the table. On the other side of the table, an important-looking officer sat on the middle chair. Seated on one side of the officer was a man who acted as an interpreter. I claim he got both himself and us into a lot of trouble with his limited knowledge of English. There also was a lady who wrote down everything we said, into a ledger.

The interpreter introduced the man sitting in the middle as the "Officer of Communication." He proceeded to ask us questions for the next two-and-a-half hours. How long were you in that lady's home? Did you take any pictures? How long have you been in this country, and what is your purpose for being here? What is your occupation? I told him of my years of service at the leprosarium in 1960, and that we just wanted to visit some friends.

After some time, he began to question my wife, Deloris. He asked her many of the same questions. When asked her occupation, she told them she was a middle school secretary. They seemed confused with her answer, and it caused many more questions. We asked for (and they gave us) an English/Vietnamese dictionary, which we used to look up words to better answer their many questions.

At one point, he asked me where our passports were. I assured him we had checked them into the hotel. In some countries it is a common practice to leave your passport at the hotel where you are staying. He continued to questions us, sometimes changing the question a little to see if our answer was the same as before. About twenty minutes later, someone came into the room with copies of all our passports. Someone had gone to the hotel and made copies for him.

Finally, the lady who had been recording everything in the ledger spoke to us in almost perfect English. She said, "We are going to call a cab to take you back to your hotel. But you need to know that you can't just go anywhere you please, because you might go somewhere we wouldn't be able to protect you." As we arrived back at our hotel, all the employees, already having heard about the "bad guys," watched us walk to our rooms.

Following is a side-story about how our God worked on our behalf. We were picked up by the police at 4:00 p.m. on Sunday afternoon, which is 4:00 a.m. here in Ohio. At that time, our son-in-law Daniel woke up and told his wife, "We need to pray for Momma and Daddy, because they are in trouble."

Home Again, Again

Needless to say, we were very happy to arrive safely back in Ohio several days later. We are so blessed to live here in the United States of America.

Life pretty much went on as usual. We had three rental houses to care for. I stopped working with real estate, taking a job delivering Meals on Wheels for the Fulton County Senior Center. I drove every day for four years. It was a very rewarding experience, serving seniors, many who live alone. For many of these seniors, I was the only other person they saw for days at a time. We had to check that the senior was ok, or call 911 for help if needed. The worst part of this job was the possibility of discovering the senior had died.

One of the seniors I delivered meals to was a lady about eighty-plus years old. She had fallen early in the spring and had broken some bones, but had nearly recovered and was walking fairly well again. Her son would check on her around 8:30 each morning, and I arrived with her meal around 11:00. One day I arrived as usual, but did not find her in her chair as usual. I hunted throughout the house, calling her name. On my way back out of the house, I noticed the walk-in garage door, which was normally closed, was standing open. She had gone to the garage to get some corn from the deep freeze. When she returned, she had lost her grip on the hand hold as she attempted to go back into the kitchen, and had fallen backward, hitting her head on the cement floor behind the car. I watched her closely to see if she was breathing, then seeing she was alive, I quickly called 911, then got some blankets to cover her to keep her warm. She rallied a little and asked me to help her get up. I told her to lie still, as the paramedics were on their way. She lived thirteen days before she passed away. The family declared I was a "hero," but I assured them I was only doing my job.

Celebrating Love and Life

About 2005, Deloris and I bought a 1958 Honda Goldwing motorcycle on E-Bay, over the internet. It belonged to a couple in North Carolina. Since I had just had major surgery, and couldn't travel anywhere, they delivered it here to our home, using a new jeep and trailer he wanted to try out. That worked out perfect for us.

We took one 600-mile trip to Illinois to a family get together. That was the only major trip we made with the bike. We did, however, ride together locally, many times just to go get an ice cream cone. Deloris was always game to go along. We had a little "speaker system" attached to our helmets, so we could talk to each other as we traveled. We enjoyed riding together.

Around June 30 of each year, which was our wedding anniversary, Deloris and I usually tried to plan a vacation: a trip to Colorado, a bed-and-breakfast, a trip to the east coast (including Washington DC), or several days in a cabin in the woods with no phone or TV.

One of the highlights was when we visited the Biltmore Estate in Asheville, North Carolina. What an amazing home and garden display. Just to think of one family living there is almost unbelievable. We took the tour of the home one day, then went back to visit the gardens and grounds the second day. It is a "must see." We enjoyed our visit there very much.

Another interesting stop we made was in the town of Boone, North Carolina. Boone is the home of Samaritan's Purse, the mission organization led by Franklin Graham. We stayed with friends,

Mick and Martha Kreszock, who I had befriended several years earlier at the Chrysler 300 Club I attended with Uncle Vernon Graber. They have become "best friends" of ours. As Martha says, "The first time you come to our house, you are a visitor. The second time you come, you are family." That's exactly how they treated us.

In 2010, we went to Asheville, NC. We visited several garden sites and other places of interest. The evening of our anniversary, I asked the lady at the hotel where we might find a good restaurant to celebrate. She recommended the "Fiddling Pig," which we found to be a great choice. There was a musical group playing Bluegrass-type music while we ate. I mentioned to our waiter we were celebrating our 48th wedding anniversary. A little later, the leader of the music group, announced that we were celebrating our anniversary. Everyone applauded.

Deep Love and Great Loss

In July of 2010, we traveled to Illinois to attend the Conrad Family Reunion in Eureka. That August, I began to notice Deloris doing some unusual things.   She went to see her doctor, who called me to come take her to the hospital for tests, "because she was not able to drive."   After taking a CT Scan, we were told she had a glioblastoma - a very aggressive brain tumor. She rapidly became unable to care for herself, becoming somewhat like a child. I was privileged to care for her at our home. The last week or so Hospice helped with her care. They are a wonderful organization.

Eight weeks later, on October 26, 2010, she went to her heavenly home. She was my sweetheart -- a beautiful lady, much loved by me and our family, and her many friends. Life is not the same without her. I miss her terribly.

Keeping Busy

In January of 2011, I was invited to spend three weeks in Florida with David and Jeanne Graber, Deloris's brother and sister-in-law. The winter of 2012, I rented an apartment in Sarasota for two months. Then in 2013, I rented a two-bed, two-bath, double-wide mobile home in Oakwood Manor park in Sarasota, for the months of January through March. It was a good winter of enjoying park activities, attending concerts, and walking the beach. I think it might be, "habit forming" as a place to spend the winters, "where it's warm and sunny."

I try to keep busy in Ohio during the summer and fall.   There is plenty of upkeep to do on my three rentals. There is also lawn care, and caring for flowers at my home. I never had to learn to prepare anything to eat, as Deloris was an expert at that. Now I eat lunch at the Senior Center nearly every day. Many evenings I eat at the local hospital cafeteria. I have learned to make a real good pumpkin pie, peach pie, and a good-tasting apple crisp.

I have always enjoyed woodworking, and am blessed to have accumulated a shop filled with some very nice tools. I made decorative shelving, and several small tables for our house or to give to family and friends.   One time on a bus tour to West

Virginia, we saw a wooden vase in a gift shop, made with many small pieces of wood glued together. I told Deloris, "I think I can make something like that!" That was the beginning of a very interesting time of designing and building bowls, dishes, and vases, using many kinds and colors of domestic and foreign woods, turning them on a lathe. I made several using the same design a quilter uses when making a quilt. Many years I entered a bowl or vase in the Fulton County Fair, often receiving a blue ribbon. One year, I even won the "Best of Show" ribbon. At Christmas time, or just to bless someone, I have enjoyed making small covered dishes to give to friends. One Christmas I made bowls for each employee at the Senior Center. On two occasions, I made a small bowl to be sold at a "mission trip auction" at church. In one vase I built, I used nearly 400 individual pieces of wood. It is really exciting to see the color and design develop when you begin to shape the rough wood.

In February 2013, while spending the winter in Florida, I mentioned to a friend that I would like to try to learn to play the mandolin. He invited me to his house to try playing his mandolin. We then looked all around the city to try to buy one, but there were no used ones available. A friend in the mobile park offered to let me use his mandolin, so I began practicing playing his.   During the summer, I found and bought one that was advertised on Craig's List.   It has been lots of fun trying to get my fingers to cooperate to make some recognizable sounds.

On any given Monday evening, there is a group of musicians called the "Circle of Friends," who get together to jam. I enjoy playing with them.

Everlasting Life

"If Christ is in you, though the body is dead because of sin, yet the spirit is alive because of righteousness." ~Romans 8:10

The "Boy from Illinois" has grown into an old man from Ohio. I haven't always done what is "pleasing in God's eyes," but because Jesus shed his blood on the cross for my salvation, and since I have been justified by faith in Jesus, I look forward to the day when I get to "go home" to heaven.

I expect to hear God say, "Well done, faithful servant. Welcome Home."

Made in the USA
Middletown, DE
16 July 2016